KEEPING THE PROMISE

A TORAH'S JOURNEY

TAMI LEHMAN-WILZIG

illustrations by CRAIG ORBACK

KAR-BEN
PUBLISHING

PHOTO COURTESY OF NASA

Dedicated to the memory of Ilan Ramon

To My Grandparents, Heinrich (Avraham) Sprinzeles z"l who died a broken man in Vienna after the Nazis came to power, and Regine (Rivka) Sprinzeles z"l, one of 4,000 Jews deported to the Izbica ghetto outside of Lublin, where no one survived. You have not been forgotten.

T.L.W.

For Jessica Silks with love. Her support and enthusiasm for my work is appreciated.

C.S.O.

The author would like to thank Professor Joachim Joseph for keeping his promise to Rabbi Simon Dasberg z"l by telling his story to the world; and to Fanny Stahl, Rabbi Dasberg's eldest daughter, who graciously opened her trunk of memories, providing insight on the rabbi's character and strength.

The illustrator would like to thank Collin Foote for modeling for the oil paintings, representing the character Joachim Joseph. Thanks also to Anna Woolley who modeled as Joachim's mom, and Jessica Silks for her help with photography.

Text copyright © 2003 by Tami Lehman-Wilzig
Illustrations copyright © 2003 by Craig Orback

KAR-BEN PUBLISHING, INC.
A division of Lerner Publishing Group
241 First Avenue North
Minneapolis, MN 55401 U.S.A.

Website address: www.kar-ben.com

Library of Congress Cataloging-in-Publication Data

Lehman-Wilzig, Tami.
    Keeping the promise : a Torah's journey / by Tami Lehman-Wilzig ; illustrations by Craig Orback.
      p. cm.
    Summary: A small Torah scroll passes from a Dutch rabbi, to a Bar Mitzvah boy during the Holocaust, to the first Israeli astronaut.
    ISBN: 1–58013–117–4 (lib. bdg. : alk. paper)
    ISBN: 1–58013–118–2 (pbk. : alk. paper)
    1. Torah scrolls—Juvenile literature. 2. Ramon, Ilan, 1954–2003—Juvenile literature. 3. Joseph, Joachim—Juvenile literature. 4. Dasberg, Simon—Juvenile literature. 5. Bergen-Belsen (Concentration camp)—Juvenile literature.
[1. Torah scrolls. 2. Ramon, Ilan, 1954–2003. 3. Joseph, Joachim. 4. Dasberg, Simon. 5. Holocaust, Jewish (1939–1945)—Netherlands.] I. Orback, Craig, ill. II. Title.
BM657.T6L44 2004
296.4'615—dc21
                                            2003010520

Manufactured in the United States of America
1 2 3 4 5 6 – JR – 09 08 07 06 05 04

"Keep this,"
whispered the rabbi to the Bar Mitzvah boy.

With a soft but firm touch he placed the tiny Torah scroll in the boy's hand. "I am sure I will not get out of here alive but maybe you will. Take it and promise that you will tell the story."

The boy did survive and made Israel his home. He grew up to be a science professor and developed experiments for outer space. When Israeli astronaut Ilan Ramon came to meet the professor in his Tel Aviv home, he saw the tiny Torah in a small ark on a bookshelf in the study. "Is there a story behind this?" asked the astronaut. The professor nodded quietly and told his tale.

ONCE THERE WAS A TINY TORAH SCROLL that could fit into the pocket of a jacket. The Torah scroll belonged to a Dutch rabbi named Simon Dasberg. Rabbi Dasberg was the rabbi of the large, beautiful synagogue at the end of the street where the Jewish butcher shop, bakery, and grocery store stood in Groningen.

He was a tall man with brown hair, a square-shaped
beard, and warm brown eyes that looked out of
wire-rimmed glasses. When dark clouds
descended on Groningen, the Nazis
forced the Jews to wear a yellow
star on their clothes. Rabbi
Dasberg walked from one end
of the city to the other, wearing
his star as a badge of honor.

"Let me shake your hand, Rabbi," the
people said as they saw him walking. "Soon the
war will be over and everything will be all right."

They were mistaken. The war did not end right away. Everything went wrong. Life for the Jews in Holland became more difficult. In time, they were sent to concentration camps, where they were forced to live in horrible conditions.

Rabbi Dasberg was sent to Bergen-Belsen. He made sure that his tiny Torah scroll was with him, safely hidden.

When he arrived, a Nazi soldier slid a dark red enamel bowl, a cup, and a metal spoon across the table to him. "For you," he sneered. Then he threw the rabbi a straw mattress and two thin blankets, and pointed to the wooden shelter where the rabbi would live.

Inside, over two hundred men and boys were crammed into rows of three-story bunk beds only two feet wide. Two people shared every bed. Rabbi Dasberg put his mattress down. He found a safe place for his possessions, making sure his precious Torah scroll was protected. Then he changed into blue and white striped work clothes and walked outside holding his head high.

Life was very difficult at Bergen Belsen, especially for the rabbi. He was sent to the forest and given a saw to cut down trees.

"Faster, Rabbi, faster," shouted the Nazi soldiers.

Day after day, for twelve straight hours, the Nazis stood by, hitting and punishing the rabbi when he stopped. With all his suffering, Rabbi Dasberg still made time to pray and read from his Torah scroll.

One day, while the rabbi was in his barracks, he noticed a young boy. "How old are you?" asked the rabbi. When he heard that the boy was about to turn thirteen, he smiled. "I thought you looked Bar Mitzvah age. Would you like me to teach you to read from the Torah so that you can have a proper Bar Mitzvah ceremony?"

The boy looked past the rabbi, staring into space. He thought of the Bar Mitzvah ceremonies celebrated by the older boys in his beautiful synagogue in Amsterdam. He had always looked forward to his own. Now he was lonely, hungry, and separated from his parents in the camp. A Bar Mitzvah sounded impossible.

"Y-e-s," the boy answered slowly, his eyes beginning to light up.

"Excellent," replied the rabbi. "We will start tonight."

Night after night, week after week, the rabbi and
the boy studied from the text of the tiny Torah
scroll. The rabbi taught the boy how to match the
words to the traditional melody used to read from
the Torah. The other Jews in the hut listened,
smiling. They, too, had become part of the secret
that was about to take place.

In the darkness before dawn, on a stormy morning in March 1944, a few days before the boy's thirteenth birthday, the Jews began to carry out the plan.

"Now!" a voice commanded the men given the job of covering the windows with blankets. Others stood watch to make sure the Nazi guards were not coming.

"Light the candles," the voice continued. The flames of four candles began to flicker.

A hand gently nudged the Bar Mitzvah boy as he lay asleep in bed.

"It's time," the voice murmured in his ear.

Rabbi Dasberg unrolled the four-inch Torah scroll as another voice softly sang in Hebrew, "Stand up, stand up, Bar Mitzvah boy!"

The skinny, cold Bar Mitzvah boy's legs were bandaged to keep them warm. With tears in his eyes, he got up and inched his way to Rabbi Dasberg. The service began. The rabbi, the boy, and some of the men huddled together. Suddenly a faint knock was heard at the door.

"Oh, no!" they gasped, frozen in fear.

Slowly and carefully someone opened the door.
A gust of cold wind blew in, chilling the air even
more. They heard a woman's voice call, "Joachim."

"Mama," the boy sobbed, rushing to the door. "How
did you know? It's dangerous for you to be here."

"Someone made sure to tell me. Don't worry,
your secret is safe. Your father wishes he could
be here, too."

"We'll get into trouble. Women are not allowed in
the men's camp," warned one of the men.

"I'll stand outside by the window and listen, then
I'll leave," answered the boy's mother, knowing
that the darkness would protect her.

The service continued. "Baruch Atah…" sang the boy as he began to recite the blessings. With Rabbi Dasberg by his side, he read from the Torah and gave a short speech.

A few voices murmured: "Mazel tov, mazel tov, you're a man now." Rabbi Dasberg then cupped his hands on the boy's head and blessed him. The men patted him on the shoulder. Tender fingers stroked his head. A hand held out a slice of bread with a piece of sausage.

"And you can have this for dessert," added another, giving the boy a piece of chocolate he had carefully hidden.

"Maybe you'll like playing with this?" a third man said, presenting him with a small deck of cards.

The boy was overjoyed, but soon his happiness was interrupted by the sound of whistles.

"Hurry, hurry," the men urged each other, quickly removing all signs of the Bar Mitzvah ceremony.

"Mama," the boy cried, running outside into his mother's warm embrace. She kissed him, and gave him a half-week's portion of bread and a pair of flannel mittens that she had secretly made for him. Joachim took his mother's hand and walked her quickly to the gate, not knowing if he would ever see her again.

Back inside, Rabbi Dasberg also had a gift for the
Bar Mitzvah boy—the tiny Torah which had been
returned to its red velvet wrapper and tucked into a
small green box. "Keep this little Torah scroll," he
whispered. "And promise that you will tell the story."

Ilan Ramon listened carefully to every detail. He thought about his mother who had also been in a concentration camp. After his visit to the professor, he returned to Houston and continued to train for his space voyage. Still, he couldn't get the story of the tiny Torah scroll out of his mind. Finally, after a few weeks, he called the professor. "Can I take the Torah scroll with me into outer space?" asked the astronaut. "Yes," agreed the professor. "Its story must be told."

And so the tiny Torah scroll boarded the spaceship Columbia with Israel's first astronaut, Ilan Ramon. On January 21, 2003, while orbiting the earth, he held up the Torah scroll for all the world to see. As he told its story, the Torah floated out of his hand in zero gravity. Afterwards he added:

"This little Sefer Torah in particular shows the ability of the Jewish people to survive everything, even the darkest of times, and to always look forward

with hope and faith for the future."

Rabbi Dasberg died in Bergen-Belsen on February 22, 1945. That same month freedom came for Joachim when an uncle was able to get forged passports for members of the Joseph family. They were released from the camp and reunited.

Ilan Ramon and the six other crew members of the Space Shuttle Columbia died February 1, 2003, when their spacecraft exploded upon re-entry into the earth's atmosphere. The Torah scroll was never recovered.

Professor Joachim Joseph watches a broadcast of Ilan Ramon holding up the miniature Torah as the Space Shuttle Columbia orbits the earth.

Rabbi Simon Dasberg's Torah rescued from the Holocaust